I am George Washington Carver

adapted by Brooke Vitale

PENGUIN YOUNG READERS LICENSES
An Imprint of Penguin Random House LLC, New York

Published in 2020 by Penguin Young Readers Licenses, an imprint of Penguin Random House LLC, New York. Manufactured in China.

Visit us online at www.penguinrandomhouse.com.

ISBN 9780593222157   10 9 8 7 6 5 4 3 2 1

"I'm open! I'm open!" Brad shouted.

Brad was playing soccer with his two best friends, Yadina and Xavier. He was determined to score a goal!

Yadina kicked the ball Brad's way. It was moving faster than he expected. The ball accidentally hit his butt and then bounced into the goal!

"Nice trick shot, Brad," Xavier said. "Did *not* see that coming!"

Xavier turned toward Yadina. She was bent over, looking at something on the ground.

"This poor little flower," Yadina said. "The ball landed right on top of it! We need to do something."

"I don't know how to help flowers," Xavier said. "But I do know where to go to find out. To the Secret Museum!"

The trio raced to the Secret Museum. Inside, they found a flower sitting on the podium.

"I wonder who it belonged to," said Brad.

Xavier pointed at a hologram that had just appeared. "George Washington Carver," he said. "That's who we're going to meet! Ready for adventure?"

"Ready!" The friends placed their hands on Berby. There was a great flash of light, and they found themselves on a farm.

"So, this is Missouri in 1870," said Xavier.

Yadina took a deep breath. "Smells . . ."

"*Sneezy!*" Brad finished, letting out a big sneeze.

They had landed in a garden.

"Oh no!" Yadina cried. They hadn't just landed *in* a garden. They had landed *on* a garden. "We came here to fix one flower, but wrecked three more. What are we going to do?"

"Don't worry!" a voice called. "The plant doctor is in."

The friends turned. Standing behind them was George Washington Carver.

"Plant doctor?" Brad asked.

George nodded. "People call me the plant doctor because I'm always helping plants. It's important to take care of the earth, you know."

Yadina pointed at the flowers. "Well, these plants definitely need taking care of," she said.

"We kind of . . . stepped on them," Brad said.

George bent down to look at the flowers. "Mmm. Yes, we'll need to quickly get these plants to my . . ." He paused and looked around. Then, in a hushed voice, he added, *Secret garden.*"

"You have a secret garden?" Yadina asked. "Does it take you back in time?"

"Ah . . . no," George responded. Then he scooped up a rusty pail, a broken teapot, and an old boot. "We can carry our plants in these!"

"Why don't we just buy flowerpots?" Xavier asked.

George shook his head. "Reusing stuff means less waste and junk lying around. It's another way of taking care of the earth."

George carefully dug out the flowers and put them in their new pots. "They can't stay there for long," he said. "We need to get them planted in my garden right away."

The friends followed George down a path through the woods.

"How come you have a secret garden?" Yadina asked as they climbed over a fallen log.

"It's where I take care of my plants. My pets."

Brad was confused. "Your plants are . . . pets?"

"Like cats and dogs?" asked Xavier.

George laughed. "Not pets like cats and dogs. But I do take care of them like a pet. They need lots of food, water, and sunshine."

"A pet plant *would* be fun," said Yadina.

Brad shook his head. "Plants just give me the sneezes."

Suddenly, something landed on Brad's flower. "A butterfly! Now there's something I love!" he said.

"And butterflies love plants," George said. "They drink from the flowers."

Brad thought that over. "I never thought about it that way. Whatever's good for butterflies is good with me. So I guess I love plants, too! *Achoo!* From a distance."

"What about you?" Yadina asked Xavier. "Don't you think plants are awesome?"

Xavier looked at the plant he was carrying. "They don't really do much for me."

"Do you like books?" George asked.

Xavier nodded enthusiastically. "I love books!"

George leaned against a tree. "The paper comes from plants!"

"How about soccer?" George continued.

Xavier nodded. "Totally."

"The ball's made from rubber," George said. "And rubber comes from plants."

Xavier's eyes grew wide. He'd never known that before.

"I bet you like breathing air," George said, taking a deep breath. "Thanks, plants!"

Xavier was amazed. "Plants make air?"

"That's right!" George said. "They make *and* clean the air we breathe."

George wasn't done. He handed Xavier a peanut butter sandwich. "Bread, jam, peanuts. All plants!"

Xavier looked down at the sandwich. "Wow! I guess plants *are* pretty awesome."

George nodded. "And since plants and the earth do so much for us, it's important we take care of them."

Xavier followed behind the others, thinking about how much plants did. Soon, the group emerged from the woods.

"My secret garden is across this field, just past those kids playing . . . soccer," George said. "Uh-oh."

"How do we get across without our plants getting hurt?" Yadina asked.

Xavier stepped up. He wasn't going to let that ball hit the plants. "I've got this. Say hello to your new plant bodyguard. Let's move!"

Taking the lead, Xavier directed his friends across the field. A ball shot their way, but he blocked it and kicked it back onto the field.

The friends were passing in front of the goal when another ball came their way. Brad ducked. Yadina tried to cover her plant. Only Xavier was ready. He blocked the ball as hard as he could, sending it back across the field.

"Nice save," said the goalie. "Thanks!"

Xavier dusted himself off. "I did it for the plants. But you're welcome."

The friends followed George the rest of the way across the field. Soon, they reached his secret garden. Flowers grew everywhere. Bees and butterflies happily flew around.

George dug a hole for each flower and replanted it. "There. Some water, food, and lots of sunshine," he said. "I think you'll get along just fine."

"Wow. You really are the plant doctor," Yadina said. "Thanks for saving these flowers."

"Of course," George said. "It's important to take care of the earth."

"I guess you're right," Xavier said. "That means we better get back home and take care of our plant, too."

The friends reached out and placed their hands on Berby. There was a flash of light, and they found themselves back in the field outside the museum.

Working together, the three carefully dug up the flower and brought it somewhere safer.

"Hope you like your sunny new home," Yadina told the flower when she was done replanting it.

Xavier found a birdcage with a missing bottom! "Dad was about to throw this out, but we can reuse it to keep the flower safe," he said.

Xavier placed the birdcage over the flower and stepped back to admire it. "It may just be one flower, but if everyone helped one plant, we'd all be taking care of the earth."

Yadina grinned and picked up the soccer ball. "That's what I said. Now, back to our game!"